# EAL in the Early

## Hundreds of ideas for supporting children with English as an Additional Language

Anita Soni

FEATHERSTONE
AN IMPRINT OF BLOOMSBURY
LONDON  NEW DELHI  NEW YORK  SYDNEY

Published 2013 by Featherstone, an imprint of Bloomsbury Publishing plc
50 Bedford Square, London, WC1B 3DP
www.bloomsbury.com

ISBN 978-1-4081-5987-3

Photographs with kind permission of:
Little Angels Schoolhouse, Hackney, London;
Acorn Childcare Ltd, Milton Keynes.

A CIP catalogue for this book is available from the British Library.

Printed and bound in India by Replika Press Pvt. Ltd

10 9 8 7 6 5 4 3 2 1

This book is produced using paper that is made from wood grown in managed, sustainable forests. It is natural, renewable and recyclable. The logging and manufacturing process conform to the environmental regulations of the country of origin.

To see our full range of titles visit www.bloomsbury.com

# Contents

# Introduction

There is much that can be done to support the children that are learning EAL in our early years settings. This book is intended to bridge theory and practice by giving an overview of the theories of language acquisition alongside practical ideas on how best to support EAL learners. The three aims of the book are:

- That it is a tool that supports staff in reflecting on their practice;
- That it is a resource that can be used to inform staff development;
- That it is a source of practical ideas on how best to support EAL.

Issues of cultural diversity have to be considered when learning EAL. This book considers these needs alongside the guidance given within the Early Years Foundation Stage (EYFS) documentation (DfE, 2012), in order to consider how best to support children in the areas of learning and development.

Other key issues such as the characteristics of effective learning, observation, assessment and planning, the environment, the Key Person approach and Special Educational Needs will also be discussed.

The chapters of this book do not have to be read in sequence. It is intended to be practical, provide relevant background and understanding and promote reflective practice. All chapters contain key messages, and Chapters 4 to 10 contain audits and self-evaluation activities to support practitioners in reflecting upon their practice.

If you are interested in the definitions of terms such as bilingualism, multilingualism and EAL, then have a look at Chapter 1. This chapter explains the changes in approaches to EAL and some of the theories and research that underpin current understanding of best practice. It also examines how language and cognition relate to each other in terms of EAL learners.

Chapter 2 is a practical chapter that looks at how early years settings can get started in their work with EAL. It considers what to do before a child arrives at the setting and some suggested ideas for the first few days and weeks. There is also a questionnaire to help reflect on practice.

Chapter 3 examines and unpicks the requirements in the Statutory Framework for the EYFS (DfE 2012) in supporting EAL. It details the practical implications of these requirements.

In Chapter 4, the prime areas of learning and development from the EYFS – Personal, Social and Emotional Development (PSED), Communication and Language, and Physical Development – are examined to consider how best to support EAL learners. There are also activities and questions for you to reflect upon, in order that you can applaud existing good practice and seek to develop it further.

Chapter 5 is written in a similar way to Chapter 4 and deals with the specific areas of learning and development: Literacy, Mathematics, Understanding the World and Expressive Arts and Design. It uses the material provided in Development Matters in the EYFS to consider the support needed for EAL learners, alongside other supporting research and information.

Chapters 6 to 9 consider key issues within early years practice, and how these relate to supporting children learning EAL. Chapter 6 starts with observation, assessment and planning. Chapter 7 looks at the Key Person approach, and how this alongside partnership with parents can be used to effectively support EAL learners. Chapter 8 considers how the environment of the setting can be optimised to enhance the experiences of the children learning EAL. Chapter 9 examines the characteristics of effective learning from within Development Matters in the Early Years Foundation Stage, and how these can be supported with children learning EAL.

Chapter 10 explores issues surrounding identification of Special Educational Needs in children learning English as an Additional Language. It also considers how best to support children learning EAL who have Special Educational Needs (SEN).

Chapters 11 and 12 are intended to support settings in developing or enhancing their work with children learning EAL. They contain activities, case studies and questions to reflect upon, in order to evaluate how well the setting is progressing and to recognise and celebrate what is going well and develop this further.

I hope that you find this book useful for your practice. Supporting children learning English as an Additional Language is not easy, but it can be rewarding and fun! I hope this book will support you, in order to best support your children.

## REFLECTION POINT

Think about the following situations and decide which category each child might fit into:

1   A Pakistani child who speaks Mirpuri at home with his family, and is living in England.
2   A child who lives in France and has one parent who speaks German.
3   An English-speaking child attending immersion classes in French, with all of his friends in a French-speaking part of Canada.
4   A Spanish-speaking child who is living in Italy with her family, as her father is working there on a one-year contract.
5   A Chinese child whose family decides he should attend an English-speaking school in Hong Kong.

## Where do bilingual people live?

If the world is taken as a whole, it is interesting to note that bilingualism is actually widespread in all countries except in the US and UK. Baker (1996) estimates '...two thirds of the world's population speaks more than one language.'

However, if countries are examined individually, bilingualism is localised and not as common. Whilst there are parts of both the US and the UK where there are higher numbers of people who are bilingual, this is limited to smaller, urban areas. For example, there are over 300 languages spoken in London and Birmingham; however, this does not represent the rest of England, which has high numbers of people who speak English alone.

In the US there are areas where the most common first language is not English–American, but is another language such as Spanish. The local society in which these people live maintains this situation as there is no need to acquire the majority language, in this case English, for the people to function successfully. There are comparable areas in Birmingham where there are densely populated areas where children may not need to speak English. This is because their main sources of communication are other people who speak the same language as them. The children speak to their parents and siblings in their own language, can access doctors who speak the same language, have neighbours who speak their language and there is even television broadcast in their language.

## What are the patterns of bilingualism?

Children in early years settings grow up in different circumstances, and these circumstances affect the way they acquire and understand a second language, in this case English. The most common patterns of language within families who are raised bilingually from birth have been identified by Langdon and Cheng (1992) and are shown in the table below.

| Language pattern | Explanation | Examples |
|---|---|---|
| One person – one language | This is where one adult in the family speaks one language and the other speaks another. | With a child speaking Hebrew and English, the mother speaks only Hebrew, the father speaks only English to their child.<br>With a child speaking French and Spanish, the mother speaks French and the stepfather speaks Spanish. |
| One place – one language | This is where there are places where one language is spoken and other places where the other is spoken. | With a child speaking Punjabi and English, Punjabi is spoken with grandparents in their house and at the temple, and English is spoken at home and in nursery. |
| One time of day – one language | This is where one language is used at one time of day, and the other language is used at another time of day. | With a child speaking Chinese and English, both parents speak English during the day, and speak Chinese in the evening. Both parents have to be competent in both Chinese and English. |
| Alternating use of languages | This is where there are differing circumstances and places where the two languages are used. | Both parents switch between using both languages depending on contextual factors such as the other people present, the topic, the location and the activity. Both parents have to be competent in both languages. |

*Source: Based on patterns in language use by Langdon and Cheng, 1992 cited in Buckley, 2003, p.155*

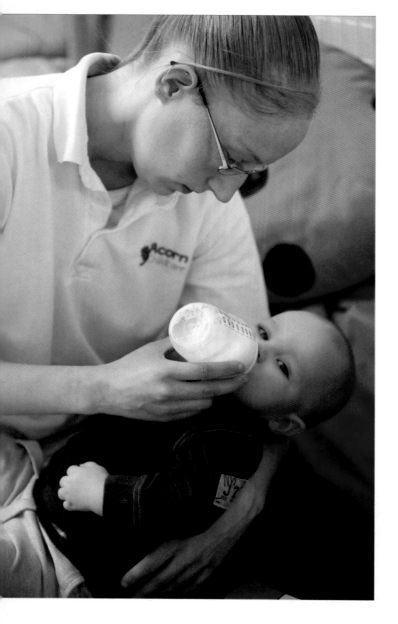

## How do children learn a second language?

There are two ways that children learn another language:

1   For some children, the two languages are introduced at the same time. This is known as simultaneous acquisition of two languages.

2   For some children, another language is introduced after the child has a sound command of the first language. This is known as sequential acquisition.

### How does simultaneous acquisition of two languages happen?

This is when the baby experiences both languages within the family from the time it was born. The experience of when the two languages are used with the child can be different. The baby could experience any of the language patterns listed in the table on the previous page. The baby could experience one language with one person and one language with another. Equally the baby could experience different languages in different places or at different times, or a mixture of these experiences. The implication of simultaneous acquisition of two languages is that the baby experiences a wider range of sounds and learns different patterns and rules of languages. This can be very different depending on the languages spoken.

## CASE STUDY

Jessie is ten months old. She hears her mum speaking in Portuguese and her dad speaking in English. Jessie recognises and enjoys the Portuguese nursery rhymes her mum sings. 'Even though she spends more time with her mum, she can follow simple instructions such as 'Come here', 'Stop', 'Milk' in Portuguese and English.

## What is sequential acquisition of two languages?

In early years settings it is more common to encounter babies and children who have already learned their first or home language to their expected age and stage and possibly beyond, who are then learning, or have learnt, a second language such as English, after that. This is known as sequential acquisition.

If a child has not already attended an early years setting, they are more likely to experience the second language when playing with siblings and other children, when watching television or when out in the community, for example when shopping with their parents. By this point the children may already know how to communicate, why communication is important and the rules of social interaction. They may also know how language works, although this is not in technical terms such as words, grammar and phrases. Children may know:

> '...that words refer to objects and events, that words can be combined to form phrases and sentences, and that application of grammatical rules can change the tense of an utterance – combined with their knowledge about communication provides children with strategies to apply when learning an additional language,'

(Madhani, 1994 cited in Buckley, 2003, p.163)

If the child is not encouraged to continue to develop their first language then there is a danger that this can lead to 'subtractive bilingualism.' This means that English becomes the child's predominant language, and in some cases children can lose the ability to communicate in their home or first language. It is important to balance a child's need to learn English with their right to maintain their first or home language.

## What are the implications of simultaneous or sequential acquisition of two languages? Which is best?

In the past it has been argued that a child who experiences two or more languages from birth will be confused and that this in turn will affect their ability to communicate in later life. It can be argued that this view is still evident within English culture. This may be one of the reasons for the England being one of the few monolingual nations.

However, research in the last 20 years has offered the different viewpoint that babies can understand and differentiate between two languages:

> '[...] babies appear to be biologically prepared and ready not only to acquire or learn two or more languages but also to remember and store these languages. To do this they have to be able to see the differences between these languages and to discriminate between them.'

(Meisel, 2004 and Genese, 2003, cited in Smidt, 2008, p.53)

Mehler et al. added that babies 'will babble in their stronger language and will show some language-specific babbling features in each of their languages' (Mehler et al., 1988 cited in Smidt, 2008 p.54). The research from Deuchar and Quay shows that even the youngest bilingual children are 'able to choose which language to use with which person but also to match the language to the context' (Deuchar and Quay, 2001, cited in Smidt, 2008, p.54).

This demonstrates that babies and young children have some understanding of their own language patterns. This is an aspect of their development that practitioners can overlook.

However, it is also important to recognise that babies and children will explore and experiment with both languages in different contexts and with different people. An example of this is when a new child is settling in to an early years setting and may have spoken Polish, the language he speaks at home, to his Key Person. This may be for a number of reasons, such as the child believes that all females speak Polish or that English is used only in contexts outside of the home such as in shops. Most important is to recognise that the child will experience confusion when his/her Key Person does not respond.

Sometimes when bilingual people are talking together they will use English utterances within the other language they are using. This can be for a number of different reasons such as tiredness, being distracted,

## Reflecting on supporting children learning EAL so that they feel happy and settled at the setting

In order to help a child to feel comfortable in the setting, do you:

- Collect information relevant to all children, for example, what they like to play with, what their favourite songs and stories are and how they like to be comforted?

- Know how to pronounce and spell the children's and parent's names correctly?

And, have you:

- Given parents an opportunity to share their wishes with regard to use of their home language and shared the policy or statement on supporting children learning EAL?

- Reviewed your environment to include pictures of families from different backgrounds, representation of different scripts and resources relevant to the child, both a favourite toy and resources of cultural significance?

- Discussed how the family would like to be communicated with, for example, email, through a family friend or a daily diary sheet?

- Asked another parent at the setting to befriend the family in order to support transition?

- Shared your parent partnership/Key Person policy to reinforce what the parents can expect from the nursery and the nursery's expectations of the parents as well?

- Let parents know that the child can bring in familiar/comforting resources from home?

- Asked about any cultural differences, for example, use of knives and forks, encouraging independence?

- Considered the option of translation, and how to go about this effectively whilst maintaining the family and child's confidentiality?

Do all the practitioners in the room/setting:

- Have a good understanding of the induction information gathered, for example, have they learnt the key words or how to pronounce the child's name?

- Need any additional training to implement the nursery policies shared with the parents?

- Use non-verbal communication well, for example, do they have a comforting tone of voice? Do they use positive expressions?

# CHAPTER 3

# EAL and the EYFS

This chapter considers the role of the Statutory Framework for the EYFS (DfE 2012) and the requirements in relation to children learning EAL. This is then considered in relation to other guidance, and practical steps are identified to achieve these requirements. This chapter endS with questions to aid reflection on practice in relation to the Statutory Framework for the EYFS.

The EYFS framework became mandatory for all early years providers from 1 September 2012. This includes maintained schools, non-maintained schools, independent schools and all providers on the Early Years Register. Thus, the scope of the framework includes those who work in the private, voluntary and independent sectors as well as childminders. Learning and development requirements are given legal force by an Order made under Section 39(1)(a) of the Childcare Act 2006. Safeguarding and welfare requirements are given legal force by Regulations made under Section 39(1)(b) of the Childcare Act 2006. The framework contains:

- an introduction which includes the overarching principles of the EYFS;
- the learning and development requirements including assessment;
- safeguarding and welfare requirements.

The aims of the EYFS were discussed briefly in Chapter 2 and are relevant to when considering children learning EAL. The EYFS seeks to provide:

- quality and consistency in all early years settings, so that every child makes good progress and no child gets left behind;
- a secure foundation through learning and development opportunities, planned around the needs and interests of each individual child and assessed and reviewed regularly;
- partnership working between practitioners, and with parents and/or carers;
- equality of opportunity and anti-discriminatory practice, ensuring that every child is included and supported.

*(EYFS, DfE 2012, p.2)*

These are important points to consider. In 2009, the EYFSP (Department for Children Schools and Families (DCSF), 2010) results showed that:

> *'54% of children whose first language was English achieved six or more points in each of the seven scales in Personal, Social, Emotional Development (PSED) and Communication, Language and Literacy development (CLL) compared to 42% of children whose first language is other than English. The percentage of children gaining this score overall was 52%. Primary National Strategy, 2007 reminds practitioners that whilst '...the skills, knowledge and understanding of children learning English as an additional language (EAL) are often underestimated. This makes it more likely that they will be vulnerable to poor Foundation Stage Profile outcomes.'*

This data illustrates a need to ensure that there is quality and consistency for all children including those learning EAL, and that all children are included and supported. The EYFS Development Matter Guidance highlights four principles that should guide practice in early years settings:

- every child is a unique child, who is constantly learning and can be resilient, capable, confident and self-assured;
- children learn to be strong and independent through positive relationships;
- children learn and develop well in enabling environments, in which their experiences respond to their individual needs and there is a strong partnership between practitioners and parents and/or carers;
- children develop and learn in different ways and at different rates. The framework covers the education and care of all children in early years provision, including children with Special Educational Needs and disabilities.

Within the learning and development requirements there is specific guidance for children learning EAL. The EYFS states:

> *'1.8 For children whose home language is not English, providers must take reasonable steps to provide opportunities for children to develop and use their home language in play and learning, supporting their language development at home. Providers must also ensure that children have sufficient opportunities to learn and reach a good standard in English language during the EYFS, ensuring children are ready to benefit from the opportunities available to them when they begin Year 1. When assessing communication, language and literacy skills, practitioners must assess children's skills in English. If a child does not have a strong grasp of English language, practitioners must explore the child's skills in the home language with parents and/or carers, to establish whether there is cause for concern about language delay.'*

This requirement will now to be considered in detail to pick out the following key messages.

1  **Providers must take reasonable steps to provide opportunities for children to develop and use their home language in play and learning at the setting.**

This means that providers need to find out about children's home languages when the child starts in a setting (see Chapter 2). Then there is an emphasis on the practitioners to encourage the child to use their home language in the setting. This can be done through:

- buddying-up children who speak the same language to play together;

- practitioners using some key words of the child's home language to encourage its use in the setting;

- practitioners encouraging children to say things in different languages, in order to show an acceptance of different languages;

- providing representations of different languages in the setting, both written and verbal.

2  **Providers must support children whose home language is not English in their language development at home.**

This means that providers have to be aware of the languages that children speak or understand at home. They also need to talk to parents about their policy or statement on supporting children who are learning

EAL. The earlier this statement is discussed with parents the less likely there are to be problems or misunderstandings. It is important to be clear in the policy or statement on the use of home languages and English in the setting and in the home, and how both are seen as important.

The following key principles from Supporting Children Learning EAL (Primary National Strategy, 2007), alongside the requirements of the EYFS, may be helpful as a starting point for a policy or statement on supporting children learning EAL. These are:

- Bilingualism is an asset and the first language has a continuing and significant role in identity, learning and the acquisition of additional languages.

- Supporting continued development of first language and promoting the use of first language for learning enables children to access learning opportunities within the EYFS and beyond through their full language repertoire.

- Cognitive challenge can and should be kept appropriately high through the provision of linguistic and contextual support.

- Language acquisition goes hand in hand with cognitive and academic development, with an inclusive curriculum as the context.

In their guidance on supporting children learning EAL, the Primary National Strategy recognises that the need to talk to parents about how important their home language is:

> *'Children need to develop strong foundations in the language that is dominant in the home environment, where most children spend most of their time. Home language skills are transferable to new languages and strengthen children's understanding of language use.'*

(Primary National Strategy, 2007, p.4)

In terms of the environment supporting children learning EAL do you have?

- Displays of words from different home languages that parents and other key adults have contributed to?

- The languages spoken by all the staff, families and children who attend the setting in speaking and in writing?

- Props and materials that encourage children to re-enact familiar events or experiences?

- Photographs that support children in anticipating the routine and order of the day?

- A record of the language(s) the children's prefer to use at home?

- Staff using key words in home language that children are likely to understand?

- Recording and play-back devices containing parents' sounds, rhymes, stories or lullabies?

- Have a setting policy or statement that explains that strong foundations in a home language support the development of English?

- Stories and songs with repetitive phrases and structures to read aloud to children to support specific vocabulary or language structures?

- A range of opportunities for children learning EAL to use their home language in the setting?

- Plan and offer a wide range of experiences for children to build their vocabulary?

## Physical Development

This area of Learning and Development is divided into two aspects in Development Matters in the EYFS:

- Moving and handling
- Health and self-care

It is vital to remember that practitioners supporting children learning EAL will need to develop the physical skills of all the children and what is good practice for all of the children is good practice for children learning EAL.

The Development Matters statements that are particularly relevant to children learning EAL are within Health and Self-care rather than Moving and Handling. This does not mean children learning EAL do not have specific needs but these are likely to be linked to how practitioners communicate with children about the expectations, experiences and activities offered within Physical Development. Therefore many of the points about effective communication have been covered within Communication and Language and relate to supporting children's understanding.

There are some specific Development Matters statements that are highly relevant for children learning EAL and these have been selected to help practitioners consider how best to support these children.

**Physical Development: Health and self-care**

| Age band | Positive Relationships: what adults could do | Enabling Environments: what adults could provide |
|---|---|---|
| Birth – 11 months | Talk to parents about the feeding patterns of young babies.<br><br>Discuss the cultural needs and expectations for skin and hair care with parents prior to entry to the setting, ensuring that the needs of all children are met appropriately and that parents' wishes are respected. | Plan to take account of the individual cultural and feeding needs of young babies in your group.<br><br>There may be considerable variation in the way parents feed their children at home. Remember that some parents may need interpreter support.. |
| 8 – 20 months | Talk to parents about how their baby communicates needs. Ensure that parents and carers who speak languages other than English are able to share their views.<br><br>Help children to enjoy their food and appreciate healthier choices by combining favourites with new tastes and textures. | |
| 16 – 26 months | Be aware of and learn about differences in cultural attitudes to children's developing independence.<br><br>Discuss cultural expectations for toileting, since in some cultures young boys may be used to sitting rather than standing at the toilet. | |
| 22 – 36 months | Support parents' routines with young children's toileting by having flexible routines and by encouraging children's efforts at independence.<br><br>Support children's growing independence as they do things for themselves, such as pulling up their pants after toileting, recognising differing parental expectations. | Display a colourful daily menu showing healthy meals and snacks and discuss choices with the children, reminding them, e.g. that they tried something previously and might like to try it again or encouraging them to try something new.<br><br>Be aware of eating habits at home and of the different ways people eat their food, e.g. that eating with clean fingers is as skilled and equally valued as using cutlery. |
| 30 – 50 months | | Provide a cosy place with a cushion and a soft light where a child can rest quietly if they need to. |
| 40 – 60 months | Be sensitive to varying family expectations and life patterns when encouraging thinking about health. | |

*Source: Early Education, 2012, pp.25-27*

It is noticeable in these tables that Development Matters statements have been selected for cultural reasons. This is because it is important as it is vital to understand a child's cultural background in order to best support their development in the setting.

In supporting children's health and self-care, do you:

- Talk to parents about their child's cultural needs for skin and hair care to ensure these needs are met? (See Chapter 2 for an example of a child and family record.)

- Talk to parents about their child's feeding and preferences so you know the food and drink their child is familiar with?

- Talk to parents about how their child communicates?

- Talk to parents about their expectations of their child in terms of independence in relation to eating, drinking, dressing and toileting?

- Find out how children eat at home so that there is an understanding of how the child may eat best at the setting?

- Maintain sensitivity to different family patterns in relation to health, independence and self-care?

In terms of the environment supporting children learning EAL do you have:

- Records such as child biographies showing the type of food each child is familiar with and how they eat at home?

- Communicate about the daily menus and snacks in a way that children learning EAL can understand? For example, do you have pictures and photographs of food and drink?

- Have places where children can relax and rest away from the heavy language demands of the setting?

- A record of the cultural needs of each of the children in terms of diet, self-care and independence?

## Personal, Social and Emotional Development (PSED)

This area of Learning and Development is divided into three aspects in Development Matters in the EYFS:

- Making Relationships
- Self-confidence and self-awareness
- Managing feelings and behaviour

It is vital to remember that practitioners supporting children learning EAL will need to develop the personal, social and emotional skills of all the children, and what is good practice for all of the children is good practice for children learning EAL.

There are some specific Development Matters statements for supporting children learning EAL in PSED, but many of the statements that apply to all children are relevant. The ones that have been selected in the tables that follow are particularly useful to consider when supporting children learning EAL.

Some of the statements selected here relate to children with Special Educational Needs (SEN). It is important to be clear that children learning EAL are not children with SEN, but that while some children learning EAL may have SEN, these are different needs. However, some of the approaches that are supportive of children with SEN are also useful for children learning EAL, and indeed for all children. This is largely because some strategies for children with SEN enhance ways of communicating beyond spoken English, such as using visual communication, for example, photographs, and these approaches are particularly helpful for children learning EAL.

## Personal, Social, Emotional Development – Making Relationships

| Age band | Positive Relationships: what adults could do | Enabling Environments: what adults could provide |
|---|---|---|
| Birth – 11 months | Ensure the Key Person or buddy is available to greet a young baby at the beginning of the session, and to hand them over to parents at the end of a session, so the young baby is supported and communication with parents is maintained.. | Ensure the Key Person is paired with a 'buddy' who knows the baby and family and can step in when necessary. |
| 8 – 20 months | Follow the baby's lead by repeating vocalisations, mirroring movements and showing the baby that you are 'listening' fully.. | Share knowledge about languages with staff and parents and make a poster or book of greetings in all languages use within the setting and the community. |
| 16 – 26 months | Give your full attention when young children look to you for a response. | Play name games to welcome children to the setting and help them get to know each other and the staff. |
| 22 – 36 months | Ensure that children have opportunities to join in. | Create areas in which children can sit and chat with friends, such as a snug den and cosy spaces. |
| 30 – 50 months | Support children in developing positive relationships by challenging negative comments and actions towards either peers or adults.\n\nEncourage children to play with a variety of friends from all backgrounds, so that everybody in the group experiences being included. | Provide a role-play area with materials reflecting children's family lives and communities. Consider including resources reflecting lives that are unfamiliar to broaden children's knowledge and reflect an inclusive ethos. |
| 40 – 60 months | Model being a considerate and responsive partner in interactions.\n\nBe aware of and respond to particular needs of children who are learning English as an additional language. | Ensure that children have opportunities over time to get to know everyone in their group, not just their special friends. |

*Source: Early Education, 2012, pp.8-9*

## Personal, Social, Emotional Development – Self-confidence and self-awareness

| Age band | Positive Relationships: what adults could do | Enabling Environments: what adults could provide |
|---|---|---|
| Birth – 11 months | Respond to and build on babies' expressions, actions and gestures. Babies will repeat actions that get a positive response from you.\n\nFind out what babies like and dislike through talking to parents. | Plan to have times when babies and older siblings or friends can be together.\n\nPlan time to share and reflect with parents on babies' progress and development, ensuring appropriate support is available where parents do not speak or understand English.. |
| 16 – 26 months | | Making choices is important for all children. Consider ways in which you provide for children with disabilities to make choices, and express preferences about their carers and activities. |

| 22 – 36 months | Be aware of cultural differences in attitudes and expectations. Continue to share and explain practice with parents, ensuring a two-way communication using interpreter support where necessary. | Consult with parents about children's varying levels of confidence in different situations. |
| 30 – 50 months | Encourage children to see adults as a resource and as partners in learning. | Record individual achievements that reflect significant progress for every child. |
| 40 – 60 months | Encourage children to explore and talk about what they are learning, valuing their ideas and ways of doing things. | Provide regular opportunities to reflect on successes, achievements and their own gifts and talents. |

*Source: Early Education, 2012, pp.10-11*

## Personal, Social, Emotional Development – Managing feelings and behaviour

| Age band | Positive Relationships: what adults could do | Enabling Environments: what adults could provide |
|---|---|---|
| Birth – 11 months | Find as much as you can from parents about young babies before they join the setting, so that the routines you follow are familiar and comforting. | Learn lullabies that children know from home and share them with others in the setting.<br>Suggest to parents that they bring something from home as a transitional (comfort) object. |
| 8 – 20 months | Establish shared understandings between home and setting about ways of responding to babies' emotions. | Ensure that children can use their comfort objects from home when in the setting.<br>Share information with parents to create consistency between home and setting so that babies learn about boundaries. |
| 22 – 36 months | Support children's symbolic play, recognising that pretending to do something can help children to express their feelings. | Share policies and practice with parents, ensuring an accurate two-way exchange of information through an interpreter or through translated materials, where necessary. |
| 30 – 50 months | Establish routines with predictable sequences and events.<br>Prepare children for changes in the routine.<br>Share with parents the rationale of boundaries and expectations to maintain a joint approach. | To support children with SEN, use a sequence of photographs to show the routine in the setting.<br>Use pictures or consistent gestures to show children with SEN the expected behaviours.<br>Provide a safe space for children to calm down or when they need to be quiet. |
| 40 – 60 months | Affirm and praise positive behaviour, explaining it makes children and adults feel happier. | Involve children in agreeing codes of behaviour and taking responsibility for implementing them. |

*Source: Early Education, 2012, pp.12-14*

It is noticeable in these tables that other aspects have been selected beyond those that specifically mention supporting children with EAL or use of home languages. This is because it is important to recognise that the ways of supporting children's Personal, Social and Emotional Development are universal.

## Understanding the World: The World

| Age band | Positive Relationships: what adults could do | Enabling Environments: what adults could provide |
|---|---|---|
| 22 – 36 months | Encourage young children to explore puddles, trees and surfaces such as grass, concrete or pebbles. | Develop the use of the outdoors so that young children can investigate features, e.g. a mound, a path or a wall. |
| 30 – 50 months | Use parents' knowledge to extend children's experiences of the world.<br><br>Arouse awareness of features of the environment in the setting and immediate local area, e.g. make visits to shops or a park.<br><br>Introduce vocabulary to enable children to talk about their observations and to ask questions. | Use the local area for exploring both the built and the natural environment.<br><br>Teach skills and knowledge in the context of practical activities, e.g. learning about the characteristics of liquids and solids by involving children in melting chocolate or cooking eggs. |
| 40 – 60 months + | Use appropriate words, e.g. 'town', 'village', 'road', 'path', 'house', 'flat', 'temple' and 'synagogue', to help children make distinctions in their observations.<br><br>Encourage the use of words that help children to express opinions, e.g. 'busy', 'quiet' and 'pollution.'<br><br>Use correct terms so that, e.g. children will enjoy naming a chrysalis if the practitioner uses its correct name. | Give opportunities to record findings in a variety of ways, e.g. drawing, writing, making a model or photographing. |

*Source: Early Education, 2012 pp.39-40*

## Understanding the World: Technology

| Age band | Positive Relationships: what adults could do | Enabling Environments: what adults could provide |
|---|---|---|
| 16 – 26 months | Talk about the effect of children's actions, as they investigate what things can do. | Incorporate technology resources that children recognise into their play, such as a camera. |
| 22 – 36 months | Talk about ICT apparatus, what it does, what they can do with it and how to use it safely. | Provide safe equipment to play with, such as torches, transistor radios or karaoke machines. |
| 40 – 60 months + | | Provide a range of materials and objects for children to play with that work in different ways for different purposes, e.g. egg whisk, torch, other household implements, pulleys, construction kits and tape recorders. |

*Source: Early Education, 2012 pp.41 -42*

In supporting children in understanding people and communities, do you:

- Make books about the children's backgrounds and lives using photographs?

- Provide positive images of all the children?

- Celebrate and value relevant cultural and community events?

- Share photographs of children's friends, families, pets and favourite people?

- Ensure children can talk about their home lives and community in both English and in home language?

- Invite parents and community members to talk about their home lives in other countries?

- Visit different parts of the local community that children may be familiar with?

- Have a wide range of resources in role-play that reflect children's lives?

- Help parents and children understand different faiths, cultures, communities and practices?

In supporting children in knowledge of the world, do you:

- Give first-hand experiences of the local environment?

- Have photographs of the local area to help children talk about what they have seen in English and in home language?

- Find out and use relevant key words in children's home languages to help them talk about the local community?

In supporting children in technology, do you:

- Give first-hand experiences of a range of technology?

- Find out and use relevant key words relating to technology so that children can talk about it in English and in their home languages?

## Expressive Arts and Design

This area of learning and development is divided into two aspects in Development Matters in the EYFS:

- Exploring and Using Media and Materials

- Being Imaginative

The Primary National Strategies (2007) guidance on supporting children learning EAL identifies that musical activities are particularly valuable for supporting language learning. Simple songs, rhymes and refrains chanted in a rhythmic way are often the vehicle for children's first attempts to articulate an additional language. Sharing songs and rhymes in home languages reinforces similarities in patterns of languages and fosters links between the home and the setting.

As with the specific area of learning and development, Understanding the World, Expressive Arts and Design, it is important to know the relevant key words to support children in discussing their ideas and also to support their understanding. It is also important to give children learning EAL first-hand, practical experience wherever possible, just as it is with all children. The tables on the next page identify some specific Development Matters statements that are helpful to reflect on when supporting children learning EAL with Expressive Arts and Design.

## Expressive Arts and Design: Exploring and using media and materials

| Age band | Positive Relationships: what adults could do | Enabling Environments: what adults could provide |
|---|---|---|
| 16 – 26 months | Listen with children to a variety of sounds, talking about favourite sounds, songs and music.<br><br>Introduce children to language to describe sounds and rhythm, e.g. loud and soft, fast and slow. | Provide a wide range of materials, resources and sensory experiences to enable children to explore colour, texture and space. |
| 22 – 36 months | Help children to listen to music and watch dance when opportunities arise, encouraging them to focus on how sound and movement develop from feelings and ideas. | Invite dancers and musicians from theatre groups, the locality or a nearby school so that children begin to experience live performances.<br><br>Draw on a wide range of musicians and storytellers from a variety of cultural backgrounds to extend children's experiences and to reflect their cultural Heritages. |
| 30 – 50 months | Introduce vocabulary to enable children to talk about their observations and experiences, e.g. 'smooth', 'shiny', 'rough', 'prickly', 'flat', 'patterned', 'jagged', 'bumpy', 'soft' and 'hard.' | Lead imaginative movement sessions based on children's current interests such as space travel, zoo animals or shadows. |

*Source: Early Education, 2012 pp.43-44*

## Expressive Arts and Design: Being Imaginative

| Age band | Positive Relationships: what adults could do | Enabling Environments: what adults could provide |
|---|---|---|
| 16 – 26 months | Show genuine interest and be willing to play along with a young child who is beginning to pretend. | Provide a variety of familiar resources reflecting everyday life, such as magazines, real kitchen items, telephones or washing materials. |
| 22 – 36 months | Observe and encourage children's make-believe play in order to gain an understanding of their interests. | Offer additional resources reflecting interests such as tunics, cloaks and bags. |
| 30 – 50 months | Support children's excursions into imaginary worlds by encouraging inventiveness, offering support and advice on occasions and ensuring that they have experiences that stimulate their interest. | Tell stories based on children's experiences and the people and places they know well. |
| 40 – 60 months+ | Introduce descriptive language to support children, e.g. 'rustle' and 'shuffle.' | Extend children's experience and expand their imagination through the provision of pictures, paintings, poems, music, dance and story.<br><br>Provide opportunities indoors and outdoors and support the different interests of children, e.g. in role-play of a builder's yard, encourage narratives to do with building and mending. |

*Source: Early Education, 2012 pp.45-46*

## What is planning?

Planning in the EYFS Effective Practice (DCSF, 2008b) is defined as:

> '...the next steps in children's development and learning. Much of this needs to be done on the basis of what (has been) found out from our own observations and assessments as well as information from parents.'

This definition highlights the role of planning as part of the cycle of observation, assessment and planning. This means that practitioners have to link their planning to what children are interested in and need to do.

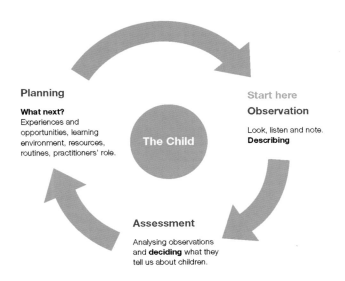

**Planning**

**What next?**
Experiences and opportunities, learning environment, resources, routines, practitioners' role.

**The Child**

**Start here**

**Observation**

Look, listen and note.
**Describing**

**Assessment**

Analysing observations and **deciding** what they tell us about children.

DfE (2012) identifies that practitioners must consider the individual needs, interests and stage of development of each child and use this information to plan a challenging and enjoyable experience for each child in all of the areas of learning and development. This should be through the medium of play. Planning should include a mix of adult-led and child-initiated activity to support children's learning and development. Practitioners have to make an ongoing judgement about the balance between activities led by children, and activities led or guided by adults. Over time it is intended that play will become more adult-guided, but remain playful. When observing, assessing and planning for the youngest children, aged birth to three, practitioners are expected to focus strongly on the three prime areas: Communication and Language, Physical Development and Personal, Social and Emotional Development. It is expected that the balance will shift towards a more equal focus on all areas of learning as children grow in confidence and ability within the three prime areas.

The Department for Education states practitioners must reflect on the different ways that children learn when planning and guiding children's activities, and reflect these in their practice (DfE, 2012). The three characteristics of effective teaching and learning are:

- **playing and exploring**: children investigate and experience things, and 'have a go';
- **active learning**: children concentrate and keep on trying if they encounter difficulties, and enjoy achievements;
- **creating and thinking critically**: children have and develop their own ideas, make links between ideas, and develop strategies for doing things.

The Department for Children, Schools and families state there are three possible levels of planning: long-term, medium-term and short-term (DCSF, 2008b).

Long-term planning is intended to provide a structure for covering all the areas of learning and development and the Principles in the EYFS Framework. For example, it can identify how the overall balance of activities is maintained. The balance may relate to:

- indoor and outdoor play;
- quiet and lively play;
- freely-chosen play opportunities through the continuous provision and well-planned, playful, adult-initiated activities.

Medium-term planning gives detail for approximately two to six weeks and tends to focus on groups of children. It may outline:

- the possible types of experiences and activities appropriate to the age/family group;
- the outline of daily routines such as feeding times, snack or mealtimes for children, arrival times, provision for outdoor activities as well as indoor, quiet time or times for rest or sleep, time for stories and for group times;
- the resources needed for room areas such as comfort/ quiet areas, home corners, messy play;
- access to equipment.

Short-term planning involves daily planning, and is focused more on individual children's needs and how these will be met. It could include the resources needed for the adult-initiated activity of cooking that has arisen from someone's birthday, a festival or another celebration. It can be the removal, adaptation or continuation of an activity included in the continuous provision based on how children have responded in the previous session/s.

## How can planning be used to support children learning EAL?

The Department for Education identifies the specific planning needs for children learning English as an Additional Language(DfE, 2012). Practitioners must provide opportunities for children to develop and use their home language in play and learning, and support their language development at home. In addition, children learning EAL need opportunities to learn and use English language during the EYFS.

Examples of how this can be reflected in long-term planning include:

- Developing an induction form that includes a language map showing the different languages used at home (see Chapter 2);

- On a regular basis, reviewing that all children's languages spoken in the setting are represented within the environment in either written form and key words are recorded for staff to use;

- Parent workshops making bilingual story sack that highlight the value of speaking and listening to children at home including the use of home language.

Examples of how this can be reflected within the medium term planning include:

- Planning bilingual story times that reflect the languages spoken and understood by the children in the setting;

- Reviewing the materials in role-play to ensure the resources reflect children's lives and home backgrounds, for example, food packaging in relevant languages;

- Labelling of equipment includes some home language words (written phonetically) to help staff use key words with children;

- Encouraging children who speak the same home language to sit near each other for dinner.

Examples of how this can be reflected within the short-term planning include:

- Adapting the continuous provision to reflect children's interests and enthusiasms, such as having more handbags and keys if these are popular and are creating opportunities for talk;

- Adult-initiated activities that build on observations, such as the discovery that many of the children play alone. This may lead to a small group time using puppets to demonstrate how to children can ask other children to play.

This can be related back to the earlier observations on Sabah, Josef and Mikey, with some suggestions for planning of next steps:

Observation:

*Sabah listened for five minutes to Fatema, her Key Person, reading a photograph book about food in both English and Punjabi. She repeated key words in Punjabi – 'roti', 'daal' and 'doodh.'*

Assessment:

Communication and Language: Listening and Attention 22 – 36 months (English and Punjabi)

Speaking 16 – 26 months (Punjabi)

**Planning:**

Medium term: Develop photograph books of the children's families

Short-term: Add relevant cooking items such as milk containers, rice and flour packaging to the role-play area. Encourage staff playing with Sabah to use the key words: 'roti', 'daal' and 'doodh' by putting these on the wall as signs with pictures/photographs.

Observation:

*Josef often plays in the home corner with his friend Mikey. They are enjoying using the mobile phones to talk to each other in mostly Polish with one or two English words –' hello' and 'goodbye.'*

Assessment:

Personal, Social and Emotional Development: Making Relationships 22 – 36 months (Polish)

Understanding the World; People and communities, 22 – 36 months (English and Polish)

**Planning:**

Medium term: Increase the space and resources available for role=play so more children can play in the area. Add newspapers and other written materials in Polish to encourage recognition of the language.

Short term: Staff to join play with Mikey and Josef and also speak on the telephone to extend children's spoken language.

## Reflecting on observing, assessing and planning for children learning EAL

Do you:

- Observe children speaking, listening or understanding their home language as well as English?

- Assess children in home language where possible?

- Involve parents of children learning English as an Additional Language in the assessment process?

- Plan to develop children's competency in English?

- Plan to develop children's use of home language in the setting?

Have you got:

- Observations in the Learning Journey that reflect the different languages the children listen to, speak and understand?

- Assessments that reflect the child learning English as an Additional language's development in English and in their home language?

# CHAPTER 10

# How to identify and support EAL learners with Special Educational needs

This chapter considers how to identify when children learning EAL have Special Educational Needs. This chapter begins by explaining what Special Educational Needs are, the guidance for supporting children with SEN and ways to identify when children learning EAL have SEN.

## What are Special Educational Needs?

The term 'Special Educational Needs' was a legally defined under the 1996 Education Act. Children have Special Educational Needs if they have learning difficulties or disabilities that make it harder for them to learn or access education than most children of the same age. Children have a learning difficulty if they have significantly greater difficulty in learning than the majority of children of the same age or have a disability which prevents or hinders them from making use of educational facilities of a kind generally provided for children of the same age.

Children with SEN need extra help, or help that is different to that given to other children of the same age. This is sometimes called 'special educational provision.' Special educational provision is educational provision that is additional or otherwise different from the provision made generally for children of their age in mainstream schools. This can include using variety of different ways of teaching or extra adult providing some help in a small group perhaps or use of particular special equipment and resources.

While the indicative draft of the (0-25) SEN Code of Practice (DfE, 2013) identifies that about 75% of children with a disability have a special educational need. It is important to remember that the disability and SEN are separate and do not always occur together in children. The Equalities Act (2010) defines disability as:

*'A person has a disability for the purposes of this Act if they have a physical or mental impairment which has a substantial and long-term adverse effect on their ability to carry out normal day-to-day activities.'*

Many children will have SEN of some kind at some time during their education. Help will usually be provided in their ordinary, mainstream early education setting or school, and sometimes this will be with the help of outside specialists. A few children will need help some of the time or all of the time in their setting. There are four categories of special educational need, which are:

1  communication and interaction (Communication and Language);

2  cognition and learning (Thinking);

3  emotional, social and behavioural development (Personal, Social and Emotional Development);

4  sensory and/or physical development (Physical Development).

Children can have difficulties in one or more areas of those listed above. These can be seen to be linked to the Early Support Developmental journals that focus on the prime areas and thinking. These materials can be found on the National Children's Bureau (NCB) website (www.ncb.org.uk/earlysupport).

## The SEN Code of Practice (2001)

The SEN Code of Practice 2001 (due to be revised in 2014) gives practical guidance on how to identify and assess children with Special Educational Needs. All early education settings, state schools, local authorities, health and social services must take account of the current SEN Code of Practice when they are dealing with children who have Special Educational Needs. This means that early education settings, schools, local authorities and health and social services should always consider the Code when they decide how they will help children with Special Educational Needs.

The 2001 SEN Code of Practice includes statutory (what must be done) and non-statutory requirements (what should be done) for teaching practitioner when assessing and making provision for children and young people's SEN. The SEN Code of Practice suggests that a graduated approach is best, as it recognises that children learn in different ways and can have different levels of SEN. So increasingly, step by step, specialist expertise can be brought in to help the setting or school with the difficulties that a child may have.

The indicative Draft: The (0-25) Special Educational Needs Code of Practice (DfE, 2013) identifies a number of principles that underpin all work with children and young people. These include:

- Early identification of needs.
- High expectations and aspirations for what children and young people with SEN and disabilities can achieve.
- Focus on the outcomes that children and young people and their families want to achieve.
- The views and participation of children and their parent/carer and young people are central.
- Choice and control for young people and parents over the support they/ their children receive.
- Education, health and social care partners collaborate for coordinated and tailored support.
- Clarity of roles and responsibilities is needed.
- High-quality provision to meet the needs of most children and young people, alongside rights for those with EHC plans to say where they wish to be educated.
- The skills, knowledge and attitude of those working with children and young people are central to achieving excellent outcomes.

These principles highlight the importance of early intervention, and this is particularly important when working with children learning English as an Additional Language where Special Educational Needs can be seen to be an EAL issue. These principles also indicate the need for every stage of assessing, identifying and supporting children with SEN to be family and child-centred.

A child with SEN may have an Individual Education Plan (IEP) play plan or access some additional support, which may be detailed in a Provision Plan. This needs to detail:

- what help is being given

- how often the child will receive the help
- who will provide the help
- what the targets for the child are
- how and when the child's progress will be checked.

If the child does not make enough progress, the Special Educational Needs Coordinator (SENCO) will then talk to the parents and family of the child to seek advice from other people outside the early years setting. This may include external agencies such as specialist teachers, educational psychologists, speech and language therapists or other health professionals. This kind of help then moves the child to Early Years Action Plus in an early years setting or School Action Plus in a school. However, this guidance is being revised and the new SEN Code of Practice may use different terms of reference in the near future.

## Can a child have both Special Educational Needs and English as an Additional Language?

It was not until the Education Act of 1981 (Department of Education and Science) that schools and settings were required by law to distinguish between having Special Educational Needs and learning English as an Additional Language. Practitioners are told not to assume that a lack of English language is linked to a learning problem and low intelligence.

*'A child is not to be taken as having a learning difficulty solely because the language (or form of language) in which he is, or will be, taught is different from a language (or form of language) which has at any time been spoken at home.'*

(Hall et al., 1995)

Here a distinction is made between children who have learning difficulties because of the language in which s/he is taught, and a child with Special Educational Needs. Nevertheless, it is essential that support is given to children to with EAL to ensure they are given full access to the curriculum during the time they are acquiring an additional language which is matched to their cognitive ability.

It is now recognised that that children do not have learning difficulties just because their first language is not English. However, it is important to recognise that some children with English as an Additional Language may have learning difficulties. Therefore the following three groups of children exist:

Three groups of children

| Children with English as an Additional Language | Children with Special Educational Needs | Children with English as an Additional Language and Special Educational Needs |
| --- | --- | --- |

However, misidentification can occur or practitioners can fail to identify children. This means that a child with EAL who does not have Special Educational Needs could be falsely identified as having SEN (false positive) and could therefore be mislabelled and subsequently taught in certain ways or using certain resources that are unsuitable. Alternatively, a child learning EAL that actually does have SEN could fail to be recognised as having Special Educational Needs (false negative) and could therefore miss out on the right help and support, which may lead to difficulties becoming even more challenging to support at a later stage. Unfortunately, there is no single assessment that is reliable enough to establish whether a bilingual child has learning difficulties or not so it remains a challenging area.

## What do you do if we think a child with English as an Additional Language has Special Educational Needs?

Ideally the child's competency in their home language use should be assessed first. This can be achieved by:

- talking to parents about how effective they are at communicating at home;

- closely observing the child within the first few months.

This will enable the practitioner to understand whether the child has a learning difficulty or whether their only difficulty is not being able to speak English. However, this can be a difficult and lengthy task, as there are complexities in separating language from learning and the process can take time.

It is important to ensure all relevant information has been collated from the parents and the setting or school. This includes:

- a language profile (see Chapter 2);

- short and long observations focused on the child's communication and language (with a consideration of the child's ability in the three aspects of Communication and Language (CL); speaking, listening and understanding);

- observations of the child in other areas of learning and development;

- the child's Learning Journey (containing formative assessments);

- transition documents (summative assessments collected at regular points in time);

- time and event samples to give an understanding of the child in a variety of situations.

In addition, video footage from the child in the home environment, with the support of someone who can translate the child's spoken word, is helpful. This information is then used to compare the child with typical development. This may be through using:

- Development Matters (Early Education, 2012) non-statutory guidance for the Early Years Foundation Stage;

- Early Years Foundation Stage Profile (depending on the child's age);

- Language assessment tools such as Wellcomm Speech and Language Assessment toolkit for the Early Years.

This will identify the child's areas of strength and areas for development. Sometimes it can be helpful to undertake observations and assessments alongside the parent, either at home or in the setting, as a child's shyness or reticence can mask their abilities. This can involve asking the parent to make certain requests of their child in home language to assess the child's understanding. This can be helpful both to gain a full assessment of the child's abilities and skills but also to help illustrate the nature of any concerns to the parents/family to enable an open discussion.

The *Every Child a Talker* Guidance (DCSF, 2008h) recommends that practitioners also take other factors of concern into account, such as the length of time the child has been in the setting and other medical or health issues, such as a hearing difficulty or middle ear infection. It can also be helpful to have an overview of the child's place in the family and how they manage at home.

It is essential that practitioners are proactive at an early stage and deal with any concerns they have that a child may have SEN, and that they do not simply assume that the child just needs more time

69

# CHAPTER 12

# Reflecting on practice

This chapter is intended to give a number of activities which can be undertaken by managers of early years settings with their staff, children and parents in order to evaluate the effectiveness of support for children learning EAL in their setting.

**Evaluate your early years setting practice through assessment of practitioners' knowledge of language development and confidence in supporting children learning EAL**

This uses an action research approach whereby the manager works with:

- staff, to reflect on their practice;
- parents;
- children.

Use the table below to check practitioner's knowledge of language development.

| Knowledge of Communication and Language development | Rate these statements 1-4  1 – no knowledge  4 – very knowledgeable | | | |
|---|---|---|---|---|
| I know about the different aspects of Communication and Language in the EYFS | | | | |
| I know where to find out more about children's development of Communication and Language | | | | |
| I know about the different age bands in Communication and Language | | | | |

Use the table below to check practitioner's confidence in supporting children learning EAL.

| Confidence in supporting children learning EAL | Rate these statements 1-4  1 – no confidence  4 – very confident | | | |
|---|---|---|---|---|
| I am confident in supporting children learning EAL in the indoor environment | | | | |
| I am confident in supporting children learning EAL in the outdoor environment | | | | |
| I am confident about supporting children learning EAL emotionally | | | | |

The Development Matters in the EYFS (Early Education, 2012) is a good place to start to support practitioner's knowledge of the three aspects of Communication and Language development, and how children progress typically within the age bands. It can be helpful to ask practitioners to describe what happens at the different age bands in terms of listening and attention, speaking and understanding. A quiz using different statements from the Development Matters can be posted up and practitioners asked to guess which age band these relate to. It is important that practitioners do not try and memorise the statements but have an understanding of approximately when children should start to say their first words, put two words together, have single-channelled attention or can understand simple sentences etc.

## Evaluate the practitioners' knowledge of their Key Children learning EAL

- Ask the practitioner to name all their Key Children.

- Ask the practitioner to name three things they know about their Key Children (including religion and cultural heritage if relevant).

- Ask the practitioners to name all the children learning EAL.

- Ask the practitioner to name what other languages the child speaks or hears at home.

- Ask the practitioner to write down the names of the parents of their Key Children.

This set of questions should be used sensitively with practitioners and are helpful prompts to reflect on whether children learning EAL are seen as individuals in the same way as children speaking English as their first language. It is vital to check if practitioners are saying and spelling names correctly.

## Evaluate practitioners' knowledge of their Key Children's home languages

- Ask the practitioner to name the languages that are spoken and understood by the parents and/or extended family of the Key Child.

- Ask the practitioner to name which written languages children experience in their homes.

- Ask the practitioner to list any key words or phrases in home language that are used by the Key Child learning EAL.

It also helps identify if practitioners know about the language backgrounds of their Key Child. The child and family record form and language map (see Chapter 2 for some examples of these forms) may be a useful record to update if practitioners lack any information about their Key Children. If the practitioner does not know any key words or phrases, it may be helpful to discuss ways of finding out key words such as using the internet, talking to parents or other family members, or other practitioners who may speak the same home language as the child.

## Evaluate practitioners' knowledge of their Key Children's characteristics of effective learning

- Ask practitioners to note down the name of each Key Child's that is learning EAL, and what motivates that child to learn.

- Ask practitioners to note down the preferred companions, activities, experiences and environment of each Key Child learning EAL, i.e. where the child engages and who with.

- Ask when the child engages in critical thinking and makes links between experiences at home and in the setting.

There are a number of questions given in Chapter 7 that can also be used to help practitioners think more deeply about each Key Child's characteristics of effective learning.

## Evaluate your practice through assessment of practitioners' knowledge of how to support the children learning EAL in the prime areas of learning

Use the table below to check practitioner's knowledge of how to support children learning EAL in the prime areas of learning.

| Confidence in supporting children learning EAL | Rate these statements 1-4<br>1 – no confidence<br>4 – very confident | | | | |
|---|---|---|---|---|---|
| I am confident in supporting children learning EAL in Personal, Social and Emotional Development (PSED) | | | | | |
| I am confident in supporting children learning EAL in Communication and Language in their home language | | | | | |
| I am confident about supporting children learning EAL in Communication and Language in English | | | | | |
| I am confident about supporting children learning EAL in Physical Development | | | | | |

Completion of the above table helps judge a practitioner's confidence. It is also helpful to ask them to identify aspects of their practice that they feel are particularly relevant to support in children learning EAL. This can be completed using the following table.

| Practice that supports children learning EAL | Example of practice that supports children learning EAL |
|---|---|
| How I support children learning EAL in Personal, Social and Emotional Development (PSED) | |
| How I support children learning EAL in Communication and Language in developing their home language | |
| How I support children learning EAL in Communication and Language in learning English | |

There are further questions to support reflective practice in these prime areas of learning and development at the end of Chapter 4.

## Evaluate your practice through assessment of practitioners' knowledge of how to support the children learning EAL in the specific areas of learning

Use the table below to check practitioners confidence in supporting children learning EAL in the specific areas of learning.

| Confidence in supporting children learning EAL | Rate these statements 1-4 1 – no confidence 4 – very confident | | | |
|---|---|---|---|---|
| I am confident in supporting children learning EAL in Literacy | | | | |
| I am confident in supporting children learning EAL in Mathematics | | | | |
| I am confident about supporting children learning EAL in Understanding the World | | | | |
| I am confident about supporting children learning EAL in Expressive Arts and Design | | | | |

Completion of the above table not only helps judge a practitioner's confidence but it is also helpful to ask them to identify aspects of their practice that they feel are particularly relevant to support in children learning EAL. This can be completed using the following table.

| Practice that supports children learning EAL | Example of practice that supports children learning EAL |
|---|---|
| How I support children learning EAL in Literacy | |
| How I support children learning EAL in Mathematics | |
| How I support children learning EAL in Understanding the World | |
| How I support children learning EAL in Expressive Arts and Design | |

There are further questions to support reflective practice in these specific areas of learning and development at the end of Chapter 5.

## Evaluate the practice of the setting by talking to parents of children learning EAL how they feel about the setting

The questions could include:

- Do you and your family feel valued here?

- What do you like best about this setting?

- What would you like to change about the setting?

- What would like us to stop doing at the setting?

- Do you feel your home language is valued here at the setting?

## Evaluate the practice and environment of the setting by observing and talking to the children learning EAL who attend the setting

Observe or ask the children:

- Where, in the setting, do they play, which areas do they enjoy using and spend time in?

- Where, in the setting, they not play, which areas do they not enjoy using or spending time in?

This can be done by drawing a floor plan of the setting (include both indoor and outdoor environments) and observing and then recording where the children learning EAL go and enjoy. This can be done on the basis of staff discussion or on observations. These spaces can be recorded with a smiley face or a tick. The spaces where children do not go or where they misbehave or get upset can be recorded with a sad face or a cross. This helps give a pictorial overview of the setting and the spaces that are working for children learning EAL. The spaces with the sad faces or crosses can be discussed by the staff as a team, to consider how these can be improved and developed. Often spaces that work well for children learning EAL work well for everyone!

This can also be done in relation to the running of the setting or routines of the day. Write down what happens at different times of the day on a piece of paper. The starting point should be the time the setting opens and the end point the time when the setting shuts. Review when the children learning EAL are happiest and record this by drawing on a smiley face or a tick. At times when they are sad or anxious or angry draw the relevant face or a cross. This is easiest to do when focusing on one or two children learning EAL at a time. This gives an overview of how the children are feeling as the day progresses and may help create a talking point for staff in terms of how can there be more smiley faces on the timeline of the day. A partially completed example is shown below.

| Time | Activity | How child learning EAL feels/behaves |
|---|---|---|
| 7.30 | Doors open – breakfast available | |
| 8.00 | Breakfast ongoing | |
| 8.30 | | |
| 9.00 | Go into our room base | |
| 9.30 | | |
| 10.00 | | |
| 10.30 | | |
| 11.00 | | |
| 11.30 | | |